Unlocking Forever

10 Keys to a Successful Marriage
Beyond I Do

By: Byron and Margaret McKie

Byron & Margaret McKie

Copyright © 2024 All Rights Reserved

No part of this publication may be copied or reproduced, by any means, electronic or otherwise, without prior consent from the copyright owner and publisher of this book.

From the Authors

Hey y'all! We're Byron and Margaret from The Beyond I Do Podcast. We started our podcast because we love each other, and we love love. After several years of being happily married, we wanted to help others build long-lasting, healthy, happy relationships. We feel so grateful for the life we've created together, and we hope others can be inspired by our story.

Table of Contents

Introduction
Picture it, Georgia, 1991…

In 1991, a mutual friend introduced us. Within a few years, we went from being new friends to being best friends to being married with a child in 1997 ("The Year It All Changed"). Since then, we've grown up with our son and each other and had to figure out what we wanted our life to be.

Byron:

Fast-forward 24 years, and I watched an episode of The Steve Harvey Show, where several couples shared their secrets for a successful marriage. One couple had been married for 50 years. When asked what their secret was, they replied, "Communication." They didn't specify what that was or how to do it; they just said communication. After thinking about their response, I approached Margaret and said we should start a podcast about marriage. We discussed things and decided that since we love love and want those who want love to have the same experience we've had, we'd give it a shot. With that, The Beyond I Do Podcast was created.

Since January 29, 2023, we have shared our marriage journey with listeners. Our goal is to be one example of how regular people can create a loving, long-lasting, happy, healthy relationship. We aim to inspire those who want the same to create their own love story Beyond I Do.

This book is another extension of our goal to spread our love for love and share how we made it this far with others. We know firsthand that relationships take effort. We also know that hard things happen. Regardless of what is happening, the relationship comes first and should be the most important thing. This idea means that whatever we experience throughout life's journey, we vow that the success of our marriage outweighs it all. At the end of each chapter, we've included an action step for you and your partner to put into practice the concepts presented. We hope these words and actions bring to your relationship the same level of success and joy that we've experienced in ours.

1

How It Started: The Foundation of Your Relationship

"For me to grow, I have to know about the foundation that came before." -- David Copperfield

Margaret:

Our relationship started as a friendship. We met through a mutual friend (who I happened to have a crush on). Byron says that he knew from the beginning that he wanted to make me happy but didn't know what that would look like. Over time, we grew closer and closer and tried to date each other early on. That didn't work, but we maintained a close friendship that strengthened over time.

In late 1996, I decided to move back home from college and "finding myself" and asked Byron for help. He did, and at some point, our friendship evolved into something more. We became inseparable and began to see each other as more than friends. We did have a hiccup at the beginning when Byron's ex resurfaced, but thankfully that situation passed. In December 1997, we were married on the 13th and had our son on the 20th. Due to all of the events in 1997, it became known as "The Year It All Changed."

The start of our relationship has become one of the most important reminders of the importance of our marriage. We went through a lot that first year, and there were many times either of us could've left. Instead of leaving, we decided that our marriage would be first, and we'd protect it and make it work, period. We reflect on that time often and sometimes discuss what could've happened and how different things could have turned out. This reflection makes us even more appreciative of what we have and each other.

Your Turn:

In your relationship, thinking about the things that brought you together is important. We can get stuck in a rut of repeated actions and lose sight of all that we have in our lives. This is especially true when kids arrive or other significant changes occur.

As people change and grow, we sometimes need to think back to the beginning and about that first meeting or date. Think about the moment you realized your significant other was "The One." What made you fall in love with the person you married? What qualities set them apart from everyone else? Reflecting on these things can make current difficult times a little more manageable.

How meaningful is your relationship to you? When life gets going, we can easily take our partner for granted, and misunderstandings can occur. We challenge you and your partner to decide that your relationship will always come first and the commitment that you share is the most important thing in your relationship.

Action Step 1 - Discuss with your partner how you felt when you and your partner first met and how your feelings have changed over time, and then reenact an early date or outing with your partner.

2

How It's Going:
Your Current Situation

"The power for creating a better future is contained in the present moment: You create a good future by creating a good present." – Eckhart Tolle

Margaret:

We are currently in the middle of our 26th year of marriage. We have four children, two by birth, two adopted, and a godson we consider our own. We still have our full-time jobs while we build our desired lives. I'm a high school teacher, and Byron works in a paper mill as a Kiln Operator. We are semi-empty nesters, and we're loving that for ourselves. Most importantly, after all this time, we still love and like each other.

As we get closer and closer to being 50 years old, we are still learning and growing as individuals and as a couple. We openly share how much we've learned about each other as we share with our listeners on our podcast. The older we get, the more we realize we still have a lot to learn. We are not where we want to be, but we are certainly farther than where we started. One thing that we know is that we are co-creating our relationship each and every day. Sometimes it's smooth sailing, sometimes it's rocky and turbulent, but every time, the goal is still the same...the relationship always comes first.

Your Turn:

Take some time to examine the status of your relationship. How long have you been together? What are the dynamics of your family? What are you and your partner's current careers? How does your work situation affect your relationship, if it does at all? What's your current level of satisfaction with your relationship? How can it improve?

These questions are suggested to help you examine different aspects of your relationship. As mentioned, sometimes we get into a rhythm with our daily lives, creating a rut. We can get complacent and let these daily tasks hold more weight than what's truly important. Make sure to check in and connect with your partner, keeping in mind that one day, the kids will leave, and you'll be left with each other. How do you want that time to look?

One way to break this cycle is to look towards the future. Talk to your partner about your lives in five, ten, or twenty years. What goals do you have as individuals and as a couple? Find ways to support each other's goals and get excited about the life you are building together.

Action Step 2—With your partner, compare major areas of your lives from the beginning of your relationship to now. Reflect on all the growth you've experienced and give each other praise and compliments for your hard work.

3

#RelationshipGoals: Creating the Relationship You Want

"When we love, we always strive to become better than we are. When we strive to become better than we are, everything around us becomes better too." – Paulo Coelho

Byron:

We come from different upbringings, so our relationship role models (and their impact on our lives) are very different. I had a traditional blended family with mom, dad, and several siblings. Although I am the only biological child shared by my mother and father, I have half-siblings on both sides. Although we weren't all genetically linked, you would never know it due to the bond we still have today. My parents created a family structure that didn't differentiate between who biologically belonged to whom. Everyone was treated equally, and that continues to stand true.

My parents stayed true to their marriage vows and were together until my dad passed away in 1996. My dad exemplified the role of father and husband. I watched him care for his family and always sacrifice himself to ensure his wife and children were cared for. I couldn't have asked for a better example of the man I wanted to be when I grew up.

In addition to my parents, I had grandparents, aunts and uncles, and some of my older siblings who were married. I had several examples of what marriage looked like and how a husband shows up for his family. As I've gotten older, I realize that some of these marriages were different behind closed doors, but overall, I was exposed to several different seemingly loving, strong marriages.

Margaret:

My parents didn't get married until I was six. I actually remember parts of their courthouse ceremony. After a rocky start, my young mind imagined that marriage would be a turning point for them and that they would have a fairytale, happily ever after ending. I was absolutely wrong.

My parent's marriage was quite the opposite of Byron's. They eventually divorced when I was 16 years old, and I was happier than ever when my mom told me we were leaving. I believe that, on many levels, my parents loved each other. Looking back as an adult, I think the problem was they didn't like each other. In terms of what I wanted from a relationship, my parents became an example of what I did not want.

My maternal grandparents were divorced the year I was born. Although my paternal grandparents were married until my grandfather died, they slept in separate bedrooms, and I never thought about them as being "married." Due to the marriages I witnessed regularly, my primary relationship role models were from TV.

We were young and didn't have much life experience when we married. We knew we wanted to be married to each other, but we had to figure out how to make it work. This was an even more difficult task because we became parents a week after marriage. Thankfully, we had extended family members, friends, and church members to help guide us as we began to build the relationship we wanted.

Early in, we started to realize that we could take advice from some, not take advice from others, and decide what works for us. Along the way, we also learned that we could take advice or try something new and course correct if it didn't give us the outcome we were looking for. Nothing was set in stone, and the success of our marriage was what truly mattered.

This process taught us so much about putting each other before everyone else and learning how to keep others out of our marriage. We realized that nobody knows everything (not even us), and everything doesn't work for everyone (not even the stuff we share). This is where the idea of communication being key comes into play. You and your partner have to be willing to open up and talk to each other about what's working and what needs work.

Another lesson we had to learn was to be realistic about what we expected from each other and our marriage. There's comfort in just doing what someone else says should be done, but adjustments need to be made when the *end* result is not the *desired* result. Societal expectations, gender roles in relationships, and idolizing others based solely on outside appearances can all lead to types of disappointment and failure in your relationship. This was when we had to face reality and realize that it is totally up to us whether our marriage succeeds or fails. We soon realized we had to be our own #RelationshipGoals and do what we believed was right for us. That was the best decision we could have made for our marriage.

Your Turn:

What were some of your expectations about marriage and relationships growing up? Whose relationship did you look to as an example of what you wanted? Who do you look to now for guidance and advice in your relationship? Is there anyone who has more influence in your relationship than they should?

It may sound hypocritical for a couple with a podcast and a book about marriage to say this, but you can't just do what other people tell you to do to have a successful relationship. We want to be open and honest with everyone. We don't proclaim to know everything, but we have learned some valuable lessons throughout our journey. We just want to share what we learned, hoping it will benefit someone. As we stated in the beginning, we love love.

Action Step 3 - Discuss your expectations before and after being in your relationship. Reflect on how realistic your expectations were and what areas you may need to adjust. With your partner, develop some of your own #RealtionshipGoals to work on together.

4

No Money, Mo Problems: Managing Marital Money

"Money can't buy love, but it improves your bargaining position." – Christopher Marlowe

Byron:

Growing up, I remember taking trips to the bank with my dad. I noticed his and my mom's names on the checks. I can also recall seeing the same thing on checks belonging to other family members, which normalized the idea of both partners sharing a bank account. I honestly didn't think there was any other way. My dad was the primary breadwinner, and I never witnessed him and my mom fight over money. He was the provider and took care of the household finances, and my mom could work and spend her money as she saw fit.

When I was a child, if I asked for a new toy, I was given a chore to do to earn it. As a teenager, I started cutting grass and washing cars in the neighborhood to earn money before I could legally get a job. When I was old enough, I got my first official job at Burger King. This progression helped to instill a work ethic and a sense of working to get what I wanted. Coupled with watching my dad and how he provided for my family, I strongly desired to work hard to ensure my family was cared for.

Margaret:

The first time I encountered an ATM, then called a Tilly Machine, I thought I was witnessing magic. You put a card in a slot, and cash would come from another. I got this same feeling when I saw my mom using credit cards. I had no understanding of bills, interest charges, or account balances. I just knew that these magical cards would allow you to get anything you wanted.

Throughout elementary and middle school, I received an allowance. Every Friday, I would get money from my grandmother. It started as $5.00 but grew to $20.00 by the time I started 6th grade. Although I had minimal chores around the house, I was regularly given allowance without hesitation. In addition to allowance, I learned early on that if I spent my allowance too fast, a little pout or whine would lead to additional money, or an adult would just buy me whatever I wanted. These actions did not translate well into adulthood.

Byron:

When we got married, we decided that Margaret would stay home with our son due to the cost of daycare. I was making a whopping $6.25 per hour on my job. We had an apartment, two vehicles, and a newborn baby to care for.

Margaret:

Throughout the years, I have quit work and stayed home several times, leaving Byron to be the sole provider. In the beginning, I had difficulty adjusting and accepting that the money he made was not *his but ours*. I actually struggled with this more than he did. It was his love and compassion that helped me to understand. To feel like I was contributing, paying bills and shopping for the house became my responsibility.

Until recently, we had one primary checking account that we shared to pay for everything. We have since opened a secondary checking account to help us better manage our money. Both of these checking accounts, along with all of our savings accounts, are shared accounts. Both of our names are on all of our bank accounts. All of the income we make individually is OURS. We do not separate our money or keep tabs on who makes what. The idea of "borrowing" from a spouse is foreign to us. We believe this can create a hierarchy that could create immense issues. Having shared accounts is crucial for us because it provides transparency and shared responsibility.

Talking about finances can be difficult and uncomfortable. Even after over twenty years, this is still an area that we are constantly growing in. We have been working hard to replace old ways of thinking and limiting beliefs about money.

Although it's not always easy, it's necessary. When we discuss money, we work hard to be judgment-free and work toward our shared goals.

Your Turn:

We're not going to lie; money can be a very uncomfortable subject. When dealing with money issues, focusing on the overall goal of a successful, happy marriage is essential. With that in mind, consider how you and your partner handle money issues. Is one partner the sole income earner? If so, does this dynamic create any unhealthy power struggles? If only one partner brings home income, it's crucial for that person to acknowledge their partner's contributions.

Does either partner hide spending from the other partner? Actions like this are dishonest and can lead to much bigger problems. As we said, money situations can be uncomfortable, but being deceitful is worse. We don't support lying in any form.

Our approach to finances is the same as everything else: conduct research, get advice, and develop a plan that both partners agree on. Once a plan is in place, adjust as you see fit. Another strategy to help you create your plan is to take an online spending and savings style assessment. This information allows you and your partner to examine each other's spending and savings styles.

Action Step 4 – Create a financial plan that both partners agree with, and schedule a time to meet and reflect on how your plan is working.

5

The Apple Don't Fall Far from the Tree:
Parenting While Married

"I don't know what's more exhausting about parenting: The getting up early or acting like you know what you're doing." – Jim Gaffigan

Margaret:

One of the most frightening times in my life was when they sent us home from the hospital with our son. I honestly questioned their sanity for allowing us to just leave with a newborn baby. I hoped for the best but did not feel very good about the situation.

Byron and I had a few basic discussions about parenting, but who really understands what to discuss when you're still basically a kid yourself? We knew we didn't want to do some of the things our parents did regarding discipline, and we knew we wanted to create a home filled with peace and love for ourselves and our children. For me, I knew that I wanted my parents and extended family to maintain and respect boundaries. We wanted their support, but in the end, parenting decisions would be solely based on me and Byron.

Byron:

How we disciplined the children was a big thing for both of us. Although we're both supportive of spanking, we both had childhood experiences of spankings gone too far. We wanted to avoid these situations and find other consequences for bad behavior.

Another important thing for us was ensuring that our kids viewed us as humans who have feelings and sometimes make mistakes. We made sure that before going too far out of anger, we'd remove ourselves from the situation. We also talked to our children about their behaviors and consequences. We even apologized to them if needed. All of these efforts were a part of the goal of creating a safe, loving environment at home.

One of the most beneficial things we've learned as parents is you do not have to be your parents. You can not like how you were parented and can parent your children however you see fit. Sometimes, getting this across to your parents may be challenging, but if you and your partner support each other, it makes it easier. And if all else fails, if you don't live with your parents, you can just leave. You don't have to stay and listen or argue.

With parenting advice, just like any other advice, listen to others, conduct your own research, and do what you and your partner decide to do. You can always regroup and shift directions as needed. Being young parents, we basically grew up with our son. Thankfully, we had enough confidence and stubbornness to ignore others and do what worked for us. And all four children are still alive and kicking! Yay for small victories.

A few years back, we experienced a shift that most parents will eventually face. Our children grew up and became adults. Just when we had gotten somewhat comfortable in our roles, things changed, and we had to do the same. For those of you who are almost there, just keep going. There is light at the end of the tunnel.

Congratulations to those of you who have already passed this milestone! It's truly a wonderful feeling.

We didn't realize it until it happened, but there is a shift in your parenting when your children become adults. At this stage, we realized that our job was more to guide than to tell them what they should do. This change was actually difficult for one of our daughters as well. She had to learn to make her own decisions and deal with the consequences, good or bad, that followed. We had to reinforce to her that we would not always be around. Overall, we love this phase of parenting and enjoy spending time with our grown kids. We also love the fact that we get treated to dinner from time to time and not just the other way around.

Your Turn:

If you and your partner have children, do you have similar parenting styles and beliefs? Do you need to address any religious or cultural differences regarding raising children? Of course, it's best to address these things before having children, but that doesn't always happen.

One of the main things to stress during this phase in your relationship is not losing focus on each other. Your kids are important, and both partners should be equally involved in their care, but your children will leave one day. You don't want your relationship to be so focused on being parents that being a couple gets lost in the shuffle. A sound support system is priceless, and when available, use it to take time to reconnect as a couple. Relive the times before children and actively plan the time afterward. Not only will it benefit your relationship, but your kids will benefit from seeing a healthy marriage with two people who love and like each other. It also makes it more difficult for them to play one parent against the other, which they will try.

Action Step 5 — Each partner discusses the positives and negatives of how they were parented. Compare your stories and decide which practices you should keep and which ones you should not. Create some basic guidelines you'll follow with your children to ensure that you are both on the same page.

6

Friends with Benefits: Benefits of Being in a Relationship

"Marriage is the highest state of friendship. If happy, it lessens our cares by dividing them, at the same time that it doubles our pleasures by mutual participation." – Samuel Richardson

Byron:

Margaret is not a mechanic, nor does she ride motorcycles, but these are two of my favorite things to do in my spare time. Even though she's not physically helping, there have been times that I've been stuck while working on something, and I talk it through with her and find a solution. Sometimes, she pulls up a chair and talks to me as I work. Although she didn't want me to get it at first, it's nothing for us to climb on my bike and go for a ride to spend time together. The time we spend together is priceless.

Margaret:

We laugh together, a lot. Sometimes, during conversations, I'll be about to say, "GIRL..." and then remember who I'm talking to. Byron is truly my best friend. I love spending time with him doing everything or nothing at all. The level of comfort that I feel with him is unmatched. He allows me space to be myself without judgment. He has supported me through some of the most challenging times in my life. I will walk to the moon and back if he walks with me. I know that we'll laugh the whole way there.

We regularly see depictions of the negative aspects of marriage on social media and in real life. We wanted to highlight some benefits of being in a committed relationship. Even though marriage is not always sunshine and rainbows, we want it to be known that there is so much more good than bad for some.

One of the most important benefits of a relationship is having someone to share the load with. It can get overwhelming between household chores, parenting, jobs, and other responsibilities. Having the right partner instantly cuts down your workload. This is also important if one partner is not feeling well or is away. With communication and compromise, you can even avoid chores and tasks that you don't like doing. For example, Margaret hates vacuuming, but Byron doesn't mind it. In their years of marriage, Margaret has only vacuumed a handful of times. Byron is the main one who does that task.

Another benefit is having another person's perspective before making major or minor decisions. Sometimes, it's hard to make a choice and stick to it, especially when you start to second-guess yourself and your thinking. Having a partner allows you to talk things out and hear things in a way that may not have occurred to you.

For us, the best part of being married is having your best friend available whenever you need or want. You always have your plus one when attending events, trying new things, or going on vacations.

In addition, you have a cheerleader to congratulate and encourage you, a confidant to talk to and comfort you, a gossip partner to laugh with, someone to support you and stand by your side, and someone to let you know when you're wrong. All of this rolled into one person.

Your Turn:

How do you and your partner cultivate the "like" in your relationship? What types of non-romantic things do you do to reinforce your friendship? We are firm believers that like is just as, if not more, important than love in a relationship. Like is what makes it easier to get through the mundane day-to-day activities. It's just as crucial to pour into each other as friends as lovers. Shared hobbies and interests are a great way to do this. Respecting individual differences and finding ways to mesh those is another way to build your friendship.

Action Step 6 – Create a Couple's Bucket List of things to do together. Commit to spending time together just to enjoy each other's company.

7

Marriage Myth Busters: Clearing Up Misconceptions About Marriage

"Understanding the misunderstanding is the best understanding ever." – Sheby Khan

We are members of a marriage Facebook group. The group is "Uncensored," so we can see some of everything there. About once a month, a new member will post, saying that the things they've seen posted make them want to remain single. If we didn't have a happy marriage, we'd probably agree.

One big part of starting our podcast and writing this book was trying to dispel some of the negativity surrounding relationships and marriage. We know there are some marriages that should've never happened, and we also know that sometimes things just don't work out. We also know that there are some very happy couples out there who have loving, thriving relationships. We want to focus on those relationships and how others can reach that point.

For one podcast episode, we discussed some of the more popular myths about marriage. We chose five of those myths to write about in this book. We hope that exposing these myths and explaining how to avoid falling for them can help others avoid them.

Myth 1: Marriage is hard work

Yes, it takes work to have a successful marriage. But we want people to stop saying it's *hard* work and begin saying it takes *effort*. Hard work has such a negative connotation, and we want to remove that thinking regarding our relationship. Using the word effort, we can view things more positively while still being realistic.

Like most things in life, you get out what you put in. If both partners put effort into the relationship, it becomes less strenuous. One affirmation we speak into our relationship is, "Our marriage is fun and easy." A harmonious, drama-free relationship is one way to ensure the home is a comfortable and safe place for all.

Myth 2: You'll get tired of each other over time.

In the previous section, we talked about the importance of cultivating "like" in your relationship and being best friends with your partner. This is a big key to making sure you don't get tired of each other or grow apart. Again, being mindful of this when small children are present is especially important. It's way too easy to get caught up in parenting and daily household chores if you aren't being intentional about your relationship.

Another big part of this is committing to keeping your relationship healthy. If your relationship is a priority, you are more likely to keep it fresh and growing. Continuously invest in the relationship by continuously investing in your partner.

Myth 3: Doing _____ will fix our relationship.

If you have a toothache caused by a cavity, would you go to the furniture store and buy a new couch? If you did, I'm sure the excitement of a new couch may overshadow the pain a little. You may even be able to lay on the sofa for a nap to forget the toothache pain temporarily. Regardless of the short-term fixes, the pain will not disappear permanently until you address the problem with an appropriate solution.

Problems will arise in relationships. Having a child is not the way to fix relationship problems. In fact, this would probably have the opposite effect. Moving to another city or taking on another job is not a way to fix a marriage problem. Conflict is inevitable. As a couple, it's important to decide to address conflict directly.

Myth 4: I shouldn't have to explain things; you should just know.

Being open and honest about your feelings can be challenging for some and nearly impossible for others. However, being open and honest and communicating with your partner is the only way that your partner can truly get to know you. It's unfair to expect anyone to know you and act on that knowledge if you aren't openly communicating what you want them to know. Nine times out of ten, your partner is not a mind reader. You can't hold them accountable for information that you haven't shared. If you want your partner to know something about you, your likes and dislikes, or your desires, you must communicate that information to them.

Myth 5: Sex will get bad, or there will be less of it.

Like every other part of a relationship, when it comes to sex, the effort you put in is directly related to the results you get out. We do want to acknowledge that there will be changes in frequency and possibly intensity when it comes to sex, especially during the times when children enter the picture. But even during these times, there are ways to make your sex life fulfilling for both parties.

One thing that we found beneficial was extending fourplay by sending texts or leaving notes for each other to find throughout the day. They don't have to be explicit or extreme, just little reminders of what's coming later. This gives you and your partner something to look forward to throughout the day and excites you with possibilities.

Sometimes, when life is really trying it, you may have to resort to scheduling sex. This is fine if it's not viewed as something to check off a to-do list. In fact, scheduling time for sex can be coupled with sending texts and messages throughout the day to make it spicier.

Finally, and most importantly, talk to your partner about your likes and dislikes before, during, and after sex. Let them know what feels good and what doesn't. Be careful not to take what you're told as a personal attack. This is not about you personally; it is about sharing likes and dislikes to improve the experience for both of you. Communication and compromise will go a long way when it comes to a satisfying sex life.

Your Turn:

How many of these marriage myths have you heard before? Did you believe them? Have you encountered any of these issues in your relationship? We will always encourage others to get advice, do your own research, and then do what works best for your relationship. The same applies to dealing with misconceptions about marriage.

Action Step 7 – List ways your relationship debunks popular relationship myths. Display your list for you and your partner to see and add to it as needed. Decide together to prove these myths wrong continuously.

8

Dealing with Loss and Grief:

"What we once enjoyed and deeply loved we can never lose, for all that we love deeply becomes part of us." – Helen Keller

Byron:

In 1996, I experienced a lot of loss. I left school, my girlfriend at the time ended our two-year relationship, and the most devastating loss was the death of my father, who passed away days before his 48th birthday. In the next section, I'll share one huge negative effect of not properly dealing with this.

During our marriage, we suffered several types of loss, including dealing with repeated runaway episodes by our oldest child, several significant deaths, including both of our moms, and the loss of close relationships. We had to learn to turn to each other for support during these difficult times.

Margaret:

For most of my teen and young adult years, I hated kissing and struggled with physical touch. This wasn't significant to me until I was married and had children. Byron is a kisser. It was confusing and painful for him when I rejected his kisses. I also found myself flinching when my kids touched or hugged me. I didn't fully understand it, nor could I really explain it, but there were times when it was physically painful for others to touch me.

Fast forward 10 - 15 years into our marriage, and I had a panic attack, which led to a flood of previously repressed memories return to me. These memories revealed several years of sexual molestation that I had endured. Suddenly, so much of what I had struggled with made sense. After working through some things myself and eventually starting therapy, I've been able to process the feelings and emotions that I'd struggled with for years. I'm so thankful for Byron's love, compassion, and support during this time.

Throughout our marriage, we learned early to rely on and turn to each other in every situation. This allowed us to grow closer in times of turmoil instead of being forced apart. We also learned to have more trust in each other. This was especially helpful as Margaret worked through past traumas. Knowing your partner has your back regardless of the situation is comforting. Having a safe place to fall and a trusted shoulder to cry on when needed is awesome.

Coping with the death of both of our moms has been difficult. Losing Margaret's mom has been especially hard due to her closeness with us and our children. Experiencing these losses together allowed us to see the strength, love, and compassion we share for each other and our extended families. We've also learned that people grieve differently, and we respectfully allow the time and space needed. We both know that grief comes and goes, but we have each other to rely on when we need it.

Finally, we are big advocates for mental health awareness and therapy. Margaret has been in therapy consistently for the past few years, and she has gone from just surviving to actually living. It's been difficult at times, but it's been worth it. Byron also sought therapy to cope with anxiety before his 48th birthday, along with other concerns. We've also had some couple's sessions to check in and ensure we're both on the same page. We firmly believe that therapy is beneficial for anyone experiencing anything.

Your Turn:

Have you and your partner experienced any significant losses since being together? Have you had any issues due to childhood trauma? We cannot recommend therapy enough. Having an impartial person to talk to and process with is priceless. And the benefits definitely outweigh the costs.

Action Step 8 – Create a list of ways your partner can support you when you experience grief. Discuss any grief or loss that you've experienced together.

Thank your partner for the love and support provided during those times.

9

Wait, What?!: Communication Really is Key

"Communication sometimes is not what you first hear; listen not just for words but listen for the reason." – Catherine Pulsifer

Byron:

As I stated earlier, 1996 was a year full of loss for me. I didn't fully grasp how this affected me until years later. As Margaret continued with her education, I started to feel threatened. I questioned whether she would still feel I was good enough for her. This led to several misunderstandings, and we began to pull away from each other. The shift in our relationship and the unresolved losses created the perfect environment for me to look outside our relationship for companionship and support.

Sometimes, the most innocent actions can lead to the most detrimental outcomes. Luckily, it didn't get to a point of no return. Everything started with a Facebook post and comment. What began as an innocent post and response quickly grew into more. After a couple of back-and-forth posts, the conversation moved to Messenger, and eventually, we exchanged phone numbers and started communicating via text messages.

Margaret:

While attending graduate school, I began a friendship with one of my classmates. I'd like to say that it started innocently, but it didn't. Almost immediately, this classmate and I were flirting through email, text messages, phone calls, and in person. Because of the shift in our marriage, I quickly allowed another person to filter in.

Even though nothing physical ever happened, I had an obvious indication of when things went too far. I was leaving work one afternoon, and I had to decline a call from my classmate because I was on the phone with Byron. I actually got upset about having to talk to my husband and not my classmate. That moment let me know that I needed to course correct.

We are so thankful we were able to work through our communication issues and learn to be better listeners and communicators. In some ways, even though these incidents helped us, we would've preferred not to have had them. Not only did we make selfish decisions, we hurt each other in the process.

We realized we needed to learn how to speak up, even during uncomfortable times and situations. One method we began to use was writing to each other. This is actually something we still do. Writing, or sending long text messages, allows us to sort our thoughts and feelings without feeling pressured to say things all at once. It also allows the recipient to read the words without feeling the need to respond immediately. In addition to writing when things are wrong, we also leave letters and sticky notes for each other to express love and adoration to each other. These letters serve as reminders of how we feel about each other.

Whatever method of communication you are comfortable with, figure it out and use it! We can't stress this enough. Please open up to your partner and let them know if something is bothering you, whether it stems from the relationship or not. Talk to your partner. Learn to trust your partner and be vulnerable. Most importantly, learn to have uncomfortable conversations with your partner. Find a way to have these talks with your partner instead of leaving things that could grow and fester to linger.

Another must when communicating with your partner is to be accountable for your actions. Take responsibility and apologize when you do something wrong. A sincere apology goes a long way. Conversely, learn to accept apologies and forgive when necessary.

Your Turn:

We can't stress enough the need for open and honest communication. Miscommunication and misinterpretation can lead to many problems. Find the best ways for you and your partner to clearly communicate needs, wants, and emotions. Learning to listen to your significant other is just as important as learning to speak up for yourself. It takes both skills to communicate effectively. Try listening to your partner without interrupting and judging. Even if what they say is hurtful or you disagree with them, if it's important enough for them to talk to you about it, then you owe it to them to listen.

Action Step 9 – Find and take an online communication styles quiz and discuss the results with your partner.

10

Youth is Wasted on the Young: Growing Older While Growing Together

"Happiness in marriage is a moment-by-moment choice. A decision to love, forgive, grow, and grow old together." – Fawn Weaver

Over the years, we have experienced change as individuals and as a couple. We have evolved in how we view life and all that comes with it. Luckily, the changes and growth we've experienced has been in tandem. We strongly believe that putting our relationship first is why we've not grown apart.

Change is inevitable. The hope is that you and your partner will grow and change together as a couple. Your thinking and mindset should evolve and mature, and so should your relationship. Even though we've had some adjustments to getting older (Margaret struggles a little more with this part), we have found comfort in knowing we can share our experiences with each other. Since this is our current journey, we don't have too much to offer, but Byron wants to point out specifically that sex is still good!

Action Step 10 - Share with your partner how you think they have improved over time. Discuss how getting older has improved your relationship.

Action Steps to Create Your Beyond I Do

1 - Discuss with your partner how you felt when you first met and how your feelings have changed over time, and then reenact an early date or outing with your partner.

2 - With your partner, compare major areas of your lives from the beginning of your relationship to now. Reflect on all the growth you've experienced and give each other praise and compliments for your hard work.

3 - Discuss your expectations before and after being in your relationship. Reflect on how realistic your expectations were and what areas you may need to adjust. With your partner, develop some of your own #RealtionshipGoals to work on together.

4 - Create a financial plan that both partners agree with, and schedule a time to meet and reflect on how your plan is working.

5 - Each partner discusses the positives and negatives of how they were parented. Compare your stories and decide which practices you should keep and which ones you should not. Create some basic guidelines you'll follow with your children to ensure that you are both on the same page.

6 - Create a Couple's Bucket List of things to do together. Commit to spending time together just to enjoy each other's company.

7 - List ways your relationship debunks popular relationship myths. Display your list for you and your partner to see and add to it as needed. Decide together to prove these myths wrong continuously.

8 - Create a list of ways your partner can support you when you experience grief. Discuss any grief or loss that you've experienced together. Thank your

partner for the love and support provided during those times.

9 - Find and take an online communication styles quiz and discuss the results with your partner.

10 - Share with your partner how you think they have improved over time. Discuss how getting older has improved your relationship.

Conclusion:

We absolutely love love. We love being in love and seeing others in love. We hope that the words in this book have helped you. We want to advocate for healthy, happy relationships and encourage you and your partner to do the same.

Until next time...We will holla at y'all!

Stay in Touch

62

Don't say goodbye, say see you later!

We invite you to join us online to share your wins, ask questions, or let us know what's on your mind.
admin@beyondidopodcast.com

WWW.BEYONDIDOPODCAST.COM

www.ingramcontent.com/pod-product-compliance
Lightning Source LLC
Chambersburg PA
CBHW061343120726
48001CB00002B/1002